ALL GOD'S
ANGELS

ALL GOD'S ANGELS

*Loving & Learning
from Angelic Messengers*

Martin Shannon, cj

PARACLETE PRESS
BREWSTER, MASSACHUSETTS

2016 First printing

All God's Angels: Loving and Learning from Angelic Messengers

Copyright © 2016 by Rev. Robert L. Shannon

ISBN 978-1-61261-774-9

Library of Congress Cataloging-in-Publication Data

    Names: Shannon, Martin, author.
    Title: All God's angels : loving and learning from angelic messengers /
      Martin Shannon, CJ.
    Description: Brewster MA : Paraclete Press Inc., 2016.
    Identifiers: LCCN 2016028860 | ISBN 9781612617749 (trade paper)
    Subjects: LCSH: Angels—Biblical teaching.
    Classification: LCC BS680.A48 S45 2016 | DDC 235/.3--dc23
    LC record available at https://lccn.loc.gov/2016028860

10 9 8 7 6 5 4 3 2 1

Published by Paraclete Press
Brewster, Massachusetts
www.paracletepress.com

Printed in the United States of America

Let all God's angels worship him.

—HEBREWS 1:6

Are not all angels spirits in the divine service,
sent to serve for the sake of those
who are to inherit salvation?

—HEBREWS 1:14

CONTENTS

PREFACE

―――――

NOT LONG AFTER HER SECOND BIRTHDAY, our younger daughter, Elizabeth, contracted juvenile rheumatoid arthritis. The diagnosis came after a visit to the rheumatologist and his needle extraction of fluid from Elizabeth's knee. "If you could just hold her down in place, Mr. Shannon, especially her legs. It won't take long, but she's not going to like this at all." Elizabeth *didn't* like it at all. And neither did I. Neither one of us was prepared for this. I held her and she cried out as the needle searched for the pocket of fluid that would reveal to us what was wrong. My tiny daughter was in pain, and there was nothing I could do to make it go away.

The prescribed treatment for Elizabeth's condition involved a massive dose of children's aspirin each day, to reduce the inflammation and relieve the pain, all the while watching carefully for any sign that the disease was spreading to other joints in her body. Monthly blood tests would also be required, because of the potentially toxic level of aspirin that would be in her system. Blood tests meant more needles, and one had been quite enough for both of us, thank you very much.

On our first visit to the local Catholic hospital for tests, when we passed a life-sized crucifix, Elizabeth walked over to it, looked up, and pointed to Jesus's wounded and bloody knees, saying simply, "Jesus hurt his knees, too."

We developed a little ritual to get ready for the needle each visit. We would stop and look at the crucifix, then go to the clinic, and Elizabeth would sit on my lap. Then we would say a little prayer asking for God's help before the nurse came in. Apparently he was helping because, though she was clearly afraid, I heard no more than a whimper from Elizabeth during each test.

One day, though—I don't remember why, I must have been in a hurry, or at least distracted—we forgot to stop at the crucifix to pray. We had been passing through a time of great conflict in the church where I was pastor, and my own worries would sometimes overwhelm me. I was in my own world that day—in any case, we went to the clinic,

Elizabeth underwent the test with not even a whimper, and we started to leave. Only then, as we were about to pass by the crucifix, did I suddenly remember. I looked down at my daughter with shame and disappointment, and said, "Elizabeth, I'm so, so sorry! I completely forgot to pray with you before the needle came." To this day, her answer lifts me inside and sometimes still chokes me up. "That's all right, Daddy," she said matter-of-factly. "Jesus was holding my hand the whole time."

What had my daughter experienced that day? Whose hand had she felt? How had God come to her? Was this actually Jesus? Or was it a kind of messenger—from the Greek word *angelos*—one who brought Jesus's "presence" to my daughter, his appearance even, and held her hand "the whole time"? I don't know. At the very least, I know that her comforting visitor was angelic. And angelic visitors are what this book is about.

INTRODUCTION

We believe in One God, the Father almighty,
maker of heaven and earth,
of all things visible and invisible.

Nicene Creed

ACH TIME WE RECITE THE WORDS OF THE creed, we confess our belief that both the world we see and the world we cannot see have been created by God. Visibility is not among the criteria for faith. As a matter of fact, Jesus commends those who "have not seen and yet have come to believe" (John 20:29). There is an entire realm of divine activity that human eyes cannot perceive—at least not without God's unveiling grace. The angels belong to this invisible world, and we declare our belief in their existence every time we say the creed. St. Gregory of Nazianzus ("the Theologian") called the angels "reflections of the Perfect Light." "Some of them," he wrote, "stand before the Great God, while others by their

xvi   ALL GOD'S ANGELS

action support the whole world." Angels—a heavenly host and servants to the world.

Thousands of years of Jewish and Christian tradition teach us much about the angels. Still, we have to admit that there is much more we do not know. St. Augustine wrote: "That there exist thrones, principalities, dominions, and powers in the heavenly mansions, I believe most firmly, and I hold it as an undoubted fact that there are distinctions between them, but what exactly they are like and what exactly are the distinctions between them, I do not know." Later in the fourth or fifth century, a writer known for his expansive and detailed description of the heavenly order nevertheless concluded: "How many ranks there are of heavenly beings, what their nature is and in what manner the mystery of holy authority is ordered among them, only God can know in detail. . . . All that we can say about this is what God has revealed to us."[1]

So, what *has* God revealed to us about the angels? Our belief in angels centers on the biblical accounts of their earthly appearances. These descriptions tell us little about what angels actually *look* like, since in their nature angels are of the invisible plane of existence—they appear in forms that are visible to the human eye, even if not always immediately recognizable. What these accounts can help us to understand is what angels *do* in God's work of salvation. Their actions teach us much about their character, and about the character of the One who sends them. As the writer to the Hebrews puts it: "Are not all angels spirits in the divine service, sent to serve for the sake of those who are to inherit salvation?" (Heb. 1:14).

There are many accounts of angelic appearances in Scripture and in other sacred texts. What follows are twenty-four of the more familiar instances in the Bible, twelve each from the Old and New Testaments. Messengers from heaven visit ordinary men and women of faith (sometimes very weak faith) to deliver God's word to their ears and to do God's work in their lives. The brief reflection with each reading is not meant to be an exhaustive study, but an aid to your own prayerful meditation on the text: What can be learned from these visitations? What can be applied to our own lives of faith? Is there a heavenly "message" for us?

Angels did not stop speaking with the book of Revelation, but maybe we have stopped listening.

About the Images in This Book

The Scriptures provide us with verbal descriptions of events in which angels appeared in visible form. Over the centuries, artists have applied their skills and informed imaginations to fill in between the lines. Their works help us take in the meaning of these events with our own eyes. They are a valuable means to interpret these marvelous mysteries. And sometimes an image can open up a new way for us to think about God's invisible work in the world. Where words fail, colors and shapes can take up the message. The images included here represent only a small fraction of the art that depicts angels in biblical stories. They are here as aids for your thought and meditation; spend time with them as you ponder these wonderful texts.

$\mathcal{S}$ERVANTS OF $\mathcal{L}$OVE

Genesis 3:22–24

*Then the L*ORD *God said, "See, the man has become like one of us, knowing good and evil; and now, he might reach out his hand and take also from the tree of life, and eat, and live forever"—therefore the L*ORD *God sent him forth from the garden of Eden, to till the ground from which he was taken. He drove out the man; and **at the east of the garden of Eden he placed the cherubim**, and a sword flaming and turning to guard the way to the tree of life.*

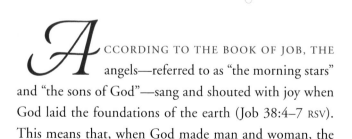

$\mathcal{A}$CCORDING TO THE BOOK OF JOB, THE angels—referred to as "the morning stars" and "the sons of God"—sang and shouted with joy when God laid the foundations of the earth (Job 38:4–7 RSV). This means that, when God made man and woman, the

Expulsion from Paradise. Byzantine mosaic. Late 12th–mid-
13th century CE. Duomo, Monreale, Italy.
Credit: Scala / Art Resource, NY

angels already existed, a myriad of invisible (except to God) witnesses on the day that a piece of hand-shaped clay first inhaled breath and became a living being. What a sight that must have been for them. Did the angels know at that same moment that their lives and the lives of these fragile creatures would be inexorably intertwined for the rest of their days?

Given this picture, the first mention of an angel in the Bible is, in many respects, an ironic introduction. What are we to make of this appearance—the cherubim standing guard at the gate of Eden, fiery sentinels appointed by God to *prevent* Adam and Eve from returning to the Garden they were created to enjoy? For one thing, this picture tells us that the primary work of the angels is to serve God. Fulfillment of the divine will is the consuming purpose of their lives. This we must always remember— angels do God's bidding, not ours.

Still, as servants of God they are servants of love, which means that barring the way back to Paradise had to be an act of divine love. Any attempt to reenter Eden on our own, to regain intimate communion with our Maker by our own efforts, is destined to be fruitless. By blocking humanity's way, the angels point to our only hope of return: the mercy of God, who will make the way himself. It will have to be his own hand—the same hand that made us—that bids the cherubim open the gate and stand aside. This portrayal of God's guardian cherubim reminds us that, as they serve, the angels' job is not to make things *easier* for us, but to make things *better*.

Even more ironic is that, actually, the first angel we encounter in the book of beginnings may be the scheming serpent (Gen. 3:1). Passages from the book of Revelation (12:7–9) and the prophet Isaiah (14:12–15) have traditionally been understood to describe Satan's ejection from heaven and his subsequent enmity with God and with all of God's works. We can't be sure, of course, but it is possible that humanity's first introduction to the appearance of angels came from a fallen one, whose primary goal was not to serve but to deceive, to tempt God's new son and daughter into defying their Creator, just as he had once done himself. Any question as to whether angels have an impact on the events of history is settled definitively here in the third chapter of Genesis.

$\mathcal{S}$EARCHING FOR THE $\mathcal{O}$UTCAST

Genesis 16:3–13

*So, after Abram had lived ten years in the land
of Canaan, Sarai, Abram's wife, took Hagar the
Egyptian, her slave-girl, and gave her to her husband
Abram as a wife. He went in to Hagar, and she
conceived; and when she saw that she had conceived,
she looked with contempt on her mistress. Then Sarai
said to Abram, "May the wrong done to me be on
you! I gave my slave-girl to your embrace, and when
she saw that she had conceived, she looked on me
with contempt. May the LORD judge between you and
me!" But Abram said to Sarai, "Your slave-girl is in
your power; do to her as you please." Then Sarai dealt
harshly with her, and she ran away from her.*

*__The angel of the LORD found her by a spring
of water in the wilderness,__ the spring on the way to
Shur. And he said, "Hagar, slave-girl of Sarai, where
have you come from and where are you going?" She
said, "I am running away from my mistress Sarai."
The angel of the LORD said to her, "Return to your*

Giovanni Lanfranco (1582-1647) *Hagar in the Desert.*
Oil on canvas, 138 x 159 cm. MV7713.
Photo Credit:© RMN-Grand Palais / Art Resource, NY

*mistress, and submit to her." The angel of the LORD
also said to her, "I will so greatly multiply your
offspring that they cannot be counted for multitude."
And the angel of the LORD said to her,*

> *"Now you have conceived and shall bear a son;
> you shall call him Ishmael,
> for the LORD has given heed to your affliction.
> He shall be a wild ass of a man,
> with his hand against everyone,
> and everyone's hand against him;
> and he shall live at odds with all his kin."*

> *So she named the LORD who spoke to her, "You
> are El-roi"; for she said, "Have I really seen God and
> remained alive after seeing him?" (see also Genesis
> 21:9–21)*

*D*ESPITE GOD'S COMMITMENT TO
give Abram and Sarai a son, and to bring
about generations of descendants from their single little
household, the long delay in the fulfillment of that
promise tempted the aging couple to take things into

their own hands. They fell to that temptation (take care not to judge them too harshly), and found a way to make things happen themselves. Hagar, and later her son Ishmael, seem to represent a diversion from God's plan, a departure from the covenant he was making with Abram and Sarai and their descendants. Nevertheless, God works with what he is given by his flawed children. Hagar and her unborn child could have been left alone in the wilderness, silently disappearing from history. Instead, God intervenes, sends his angel, and a new nation is born.

Bereft of companionship and cast forth from the only family she knew, Hagar was comforted and instructed by the angel of the Lord, who later was sent also to save Ishmael's life (see Gen. 21). This is actually the first time that the word *angel* appears in the Bible. The word *angel* means "messenger," and the message of this angel came in three ways, all having to do with the essential role of angels. First, the angel asked a question of Hagar—"Where have you come from and where are you going?"—as if the angel didn't already know the answer. (Remember, this was the same method used by the fallen angel too, when he first came to Eve: "Did God say . . . ?") It appears that this question was designed to begin a conversation with Hagar who, at that point, probably did not realize that the person she was talking with was a messenger from heaven. Apparently, angels are able to converse with those to whom they are sent. They are bringing a message, but they can listen as well.

Second, the angel makes a command: return. Telling Hagar to go back to her mistress and to submit to her, unfair as these instructions may be, seems to be the main point of his intervention. Hagar was headed in the wrong direction. The angel was sent to set her back on course. Third, on behalf of the One who sent him, the angel makes a commitment to Hagar: "I will greatly multiply your descendants." Hagar will return home, now with a divine promise in her heart to keep company with the child in her womb.

Conversation, command, commitment—as messengers of God, angels have the ability to bring a wide array of methods to their task, and we will encounter these methods as we read of other angelic appearances. In this case, they all worked together to prevent Hagar from taking a very wrong turn in her life's direction. We are never too far from home to be found by the angel of the Lord.

The Three Angels, detail of *The Hospitality of Abraham and the Sacrifice of Isaac,* 6th century (mosaic) (see 154709), Byzantine School, (6th century) / San Vitale, Ravenna, Italy / Bridgeman Images

$\mathcal{E}$NTERTAINING $\mathcal{A}$NGELS

Genesis 18:1–8

*The LORD appeared to Abraham by the oaks of
Mamre, as he sat at the entrance of his tent in the
heat of the day.* **He looked up and saw three men
standing near him.** *When he saw them, he ran from
the tent entrance to meet them, and bowed down to
the ground. He said, "My lord, if I find favor with
you, do not pass by your servant. Let a little water be
brought, and wash your feet, and rest yourselves under
the tree. Let me bring a little bread, that you may
refresh yourselves, and after that you may pass on—
since you have come to your servant." So they said,
"Do as you have said." And Abraham hastened into
the tent to Sarah, and said, "Make ready quickly three
measures of choice flour, knead it, and make cakes."
Abraham ran to the herd, and took a calf, tender
and good, and gave it to the servant, who hastened to
prepare it. Then he took curds and milk and the calf
that he had prepared, and set it before them; and he
stood by them under the tree while they ate.*

*G*OD HAD ALREADY SPOKEN TO ABRAHAM four times: calling him out of Ur, making a covenant with him for the land of Canaan, promising him a son, foretelling that generations of descendants would call him "Father." In each case, the Bible simply says that the Lord spoke to Abraham, or came to him in a vision. On this occasion, the message is brought to Abraham by three "men." The triune image evokes the Trinity, and though the Judaic mind would not have interpreted the text in this way, the writer himself identifies the appearance as "the Lord."

When the Bible speaks of "the angel of the Lord," the specific meaning is not always clear. Is it an angel *from* the Lord? Is it the person of the Lord God appearing in human form? Is it something else, altogether different and unique? For the purposes of these reflections, we are not trying to parse out this phrase too finely. What is clear is that, when either "an angel" or "the angel of the Lord" visits one of God's people, a direct connection is made between heaven and earth. Angels bring the message and the presence of God into the lives of human beings, correcting human error, strengthening human weaknesses, answering human need. Whoever these beings are, they appear on behalf of God and for the benefit of people. In this case, it took three of them to get the message across.

On the mosaic walls of San Vitale, a fourth-century church in Ravenna, Italy, this scene is depicted as three men sitting at a table, upon which are three loaves of bread, each marked with a cross. The Eucharistic meaning is unmistakable. This is the "bread of the angels" (*panis angelicus*; see Ps. 78:25), and even as they are hosting the event, Abraham and Sarah are also the guests. Abraham may have invited the men to supper, but the real invitation was extended by God, who was asking Abraham and Sarah to be part of his divine plan. The sacred meal they share, like every celebration of the Lord's Supper, is a foretaste of that plan's fulfillment. It is a meal of true communion between heaven and earth.

In one of his sermons, John Chrysostom said that, because Abraham himself was a citizen of heaven and thereby a stranger on earth (see Heb. 11:13–16), he was ready to entertain strangers with cheerfulness and generosity. The "strangers" Abraham welcomes—as is the case with all angels—are themselves ready, cheerful, and generous. They dutifully sit and eat what is set before them, then fulfill their angelic function by bringing a message from heaven to earth: "Is anything too wonderful for the Lord? At the set time I will return to you, in due season, and Sarah shall have a son" (Gen. 18:14). As with Hagar before, and centuries later in a tiny village called Nazareth, an angel announces that a child will be born.

Angels Are Never Too Late

Genesis 22:9–14

*When they reached the place God had told him
about, Abraham built an altar there and arranged
the wood on it. He bound his son Isaac and laid him
on the altar, on top of the wood. Then he reached
out his hand and took the knife to slay his son. **But
the angel of the Lord called out to him from
heaven, "Abraham! Abraham!"***

"Here I am," he replied.

*"Do not lay a hand on the boy," he said. "Do
not do anything to him. Now I know that you fear
God, because you have not withheld from me your
son, your only son." Abraham looked up and there in a
thicket he saw a ram caught by its horns. He went over
and took the ram and sacrificed it as a burnt offering
instead of his son. So Abraham called that place
The Lord Will Provide. And to this day it is said, "On
the mountain of the Lord it will be provided." (NIV)*

*H*ERE IS AN UNMISTAKABLE EXAMPLE of heaven's perfect sense of timing, and of the split-second readiness of God's angels to act on behalf of God's servants. Since the time of Shakespeare, to arrive "in the nick of time" has meant to be in precisely the right place at precisely the right time, neither too soon nor too late. Virtually every artistic depiction of this scene shows Abraham wielding a knife, his arm raised above the prone and helpless Isaac, about to inflict the violent, mortal blow that will take the life of his only son. Just at that moment, as if emerging from outside the frame or jumping up from behind a tree, an angel appears, reaching forth and withholding Abraham's arm, strong enough to prevent him from plunging the knife.

Consider, for example, the famous painting by Rembrandt. Abraham forcefully holds down his bound son atop the wood of the fire, covering his face and pushing his head back. The whiteness of Isaac's neck and chest draws

The Sacrifice of Abraham (1635) Oil on Canvas.
Rembrandt Harmensz van Rijn (1606-1669)
Hermitage, St. Petersburg, Russia
Photo Credit : Erich Lessing/ Art Resource, NY

the eye of the viewer to this image of total exposure and vulnerability. Isaac is powerless to resist as Abraham readies to kill him. While the tragic outcome seems inevitable in what appears at the bottom half of the painting, something equally active but entirely different is happening in the upper half of the scene. Suddenly (in the nick of time) an angel appears out of nowhere. While Abraham grips his son's face with one hand, the angel takes hold of Abraham's other wrist, forcing him to release the knife he is wielding. The artist depicts the instrument of death in midair, the blade's potential for destroying still apparent in its shimmer as it falls. The young Isaac doesn't know it yet, but he is saved. Meanwhile, the light on Abraham's face reveals a look of both wonder and relief: "Could it be that I, too, am saved?"

The Scriptures say nothing about any of this action, only that the angel *called* to Abraham "from heaven" and that Abraham immediately stopped what he was doing. But, in pictorial form, artists present to us the same message: the angels of the Lord are ready to act with precision and swiftness. They can come into our presence invited (as in the previous story of Abraham from Genesis 18) or uninvited, and they can move with such speed that their actions catch us unawares. Their hands are always at the ready to serve as God's hands in the world. And when they do, they always succeed in their task. "Angels are powerful and quick to do God's will," wrote John of Damascus. "Their nature is so speedy that, as soon as the divine glance orders them to go somewhere, immediately they are there." It's a good thing! Sometimes they keep us from harm; perhaps just as often they keep us from *doing* harm. In either case, they are never too late.

Jacob's Ladder, c.1490 (oil on panel) French School, (15th century)
Credit: Musee du Petit Palais, Avignon, France/Bridgeman Images

Heaven to Earth to Heaven

Genesis 28:10–17

Jacob left Beer-sheba and went toward Haran. He came to a certain place and stayed there for the night, because the sun had set. Taking one of the stones of the place, he put it under his head and lay down in that place. And he dreamed that there was a ladder set up on the earth, the top of it reaching to heaven; **and the angels of God were ascending and descending on it.** *And the* LORD *stood beside him and said, "I am the* LORD, *the God of Abraham your father and the God of Isaac; the land on which you lie I will give to you and to your offspring; and your offspring shall be like the dust of the earth, and you shall spread abroad to the west and to the east and to the north and to the south; and all the families of the earth shall be blessed in you and in your offspring. Know that I am with you and will keep you wherever you go, and will bring you back to this land; for I will not leave you until I have done what I have promised you." Then*

Jacob woke from his sleep and said, "Surely the LORD *is in this place—and I did not know it!" And he was afraid, and said, "How awesome is this place! This is none other than the house of God, and this is the gate of heaven."*

*J*ACOB CALLS THE PLACE WHERE HE SLEPT the "house of God" (Bethel) and "gate of heaven" because of the vision he beheld there in the dark of the night. Remember, he was leaving his father's house for the first time, fleeing from his brother Esau, and probably hoped for a peaceful night's rest. Instead, while his eyes are closed in sleep, his soul is opened to the revelation of God, and what he sees astonishes him—a direct passage between heaven and earth.

In some Jewish writings, the place where Jacob lay down his head is identified as the same place from which God made the earth and where God "stood" when he formed the body of Adam. Generations after Jacob, that ground would serve as the foundation for the Holy of Holies in the temple. It is associated with Mount Moriah, the place where Abraham went to sacrifice Isaac and that, today, is the floor of the Dome of the Rock in Jerusalem. On the night Jacob stopped to rest, his vision of the coming and going of angels revealed to him that he was camping on holy ground. Here, the foundation stone of all creation and the stepping stone to the Creator were one and the same.

Ascending and descending. This is an image of the never-ceasing mission of God's angels. On the one hand, the gate of paradise barred to humans appears open to the angels, who ascend the ladder freely to present themselves before God. Like us, the angels were created to live in God's presence, and they return there whenever their earthly work is completed. On the other hand, the angels descending the ladder represent for Jacob God's unhindered access to earth. It is as if Jacob's vision is expanded for a moment and he is allowed to see something usually invisible, but which is taking place all the time—heaven's messengers are *always* coming to earth's aid. Their access to us is as immediate and unrestricted as their access to God. Gregory the Great says it is as if angels can be in two places at the same time—they always behold the Father's face, and they are always coming to us. At one and the same time they are sent from God, yet they remain with God.

The angels tell us that heaven and earth are not completely separated after all. There is a particular "route" that connects them, and on that mysterious night Jacob found himself at its entrance. We know the Way as well. Early in his ministry, before his followers began to perceive who he really was, Jesus said, "Very truly, I tell you, you will see heaven opened and the angels of God ascending and descending upon the Son of Man" (John 1:51). In the Son of God there is a permanent ladder "set up on the earth, and the top of it reaches to heaven."

$\mathcal{W}$HEN $\mathcal{W}$OUNDING $\mathcal{I}$S $\mathcal{H}$EALING

Genesis 32:22–30

The same night [Jacob] got up and took his two wives, his two maids, and his eleven children, and crossed the ford of the Jabbok. He took them and sent them across the stream, and likewise everything that he had. **Jacob was left alone; and a man wrestled with him until daybreak.** *When the man saw that he did not prevail against Jacob, he struck him on the hip socket; and Jacob's hip was put out of joint as he wrestled with him. Then he said, "Let me go, for the day is breaking." But Jacob said, "I will not let you go, unless you bless me." So he said to him, "What is your name?" And he said, "Jacob." Then the man said, "You shall no longer be called Jacob, but Israel, for you have striven with God and with humans, and have prevailed." Then Jacob asked him, "Please tell me your name." But he said, "Why is it that you ask my name?" And there he blessed him. So Jacob called the place Peniel, saying,*

Eugene Delacroix (1798-1863)
Jacob Wrestling with the Angel, detail. 1850. St. Sulpice, Paris, France Photo
Credit: Scala / Art Resource, NY

"For I have seen God face to face, and yet my life is preserved."

*W*E STAY WITH JACOB FOR ANOTHER night's visitation. It is many years since his dream at Bethel, but once again he is traveling, this time on his way back home. He is very much afraid of meeting up with his brother, Esau, whom he last saw after tricking him out of his inheritance and his father's blessing. Since that time things have gone well for Jacob, though thanks in part to his continued scheming. His efforts have gained for him great wealth, and also the distrust of others. No wonder he himself is so untrusting. Still, Jacob returns home with a retinue of family, servants, and flocks, by every apparent measure seeming to be a model of success. He is even met by a vast army of angels when he first sets out, an encounter that perhaps was less a greeting than a solemn harbinger of what was to come (Gen. 32:1–2).

Who, then, was this "stranger" who came to Jacob in the night? The Bible simply says that it was a "man," but we already know that God's angels sometimes take human form in order to make themselves presentable to human eyes. In this case, it was more than the face and the voice of an angel that Jacob encountered. This was a visitation with muscle.

It is interesting that this story is usually identified as Jacob wrestling with the angel. In fact, Jacob does wrestle and actually prevails in the contest, holding fast to his not-unfriendly opponent until he obtains a reward. But the story could just as easily be named "The Angel of God Comes to Wrestle with Jacob," for it seems evident that this is precisely what the angel came to do. God is apparently not above taking us on, face to face, and arm to arm.

What must the scene have been like in heaven's courts? Such speculation is always just that—speculation—but can we imagine hearing something like this: "My messenger, I have a particularly dirty job for you tonight. Don't wear anything you are afraid of tearing. As you know, my servant Jacob, whom I love, is very cunning and strong in soul; he has succeeded in getting his way in almost everything he sets out to do. He does not yet know the depth of his own helplessness. But, tonight, almost for the first time, he is afraid. And he is alone. The time has come for him to learn an important lesson. Go meet him. When you see him, say nothing, but wrestle him to the ground. You may wound him—you *must* wound him—but you must also let him think that he has won the match. In truth, he will know that he is weaker than you, and so he will ask you for my blessing. Give it to him, generously. Thanks to what you are about to do, he will be made ready for what lies ahead."

DRAWING US TO
THE FIRE
Exodus 3:1–6

*Moses was keeping the flock of his father-in-law
Jethro, the priest of Midian; he led his flock beyond the
wilderness, and came to Horeb, the mountain of God.*
***There the angel of the LORD appeared to him in a
flame of fire out of a bush;*** *he looked, and the bush
was blazing, yet it was not consumed. Then Moses
said, "I must turn aside and look at this great sight,
and see why the bush is not burned up." When the
LORD saw that he had turned aside to see, God called
to him out of the bush, "Moses, Moses!" And he said,
"Here I am." Then he said, "Come no closer! Remove
the sandals from your feet, for the place on which you
are standing is holy ground." He said further, "I am
the God of your father, the God of Abraham, the God
of Isaac, and the God of Jacob." And Moses hid his
face, for he was afraid to look at God.*

Moses before the Burning Bush, Room of Heliodorus, Vatican
Museum (photo) / Godong / UIG / Bridgeman Images

*I*N THIS CASE, GOD'S ANGEL APPEARS under the most ordinary of circumstances, as Moses is going about his day's work of herding sheep. The encounter itself, however, is anything but ordinary. The voice of God, an angel, flames of fire, and a common thorn bush that, while ablaze, nevertheless remains unscorched: these are not everyday occurrences. And while we will probably never experience anything quite so dramatic, we can learn a great deal from this event.

The sunrise over the Midian wilderness gave Moses no clue that his world was about to be upended. No sign appeared in the sky to prepare him for an impending miracle. The countryside was the same; the bleating of the sheep was the same; Moses's duties were the same. It was a typical day but for one thing: it was God's appointed day to send his angel to meet with Moses. In order to do so, God had to get his attention.

"I must turn aside and look at this great sight," said Moses when he saw the bush all aflame. But what if Moses had been "too busy" to turn? What if he thought his schedule was too tight to fit in such a diversion? What if he were so busy living his typical day that he would not allow his focus to be interrupted? Moses's experience tells us that God will do what he must to snap us out of our lethargy and "normalcy" in order to speak to us. Could it be that some of the unexpected—even unwelcome—intrusions in our day are really "angelic" fireworks meant to make us step off our well-worn path long enough to watch and to listen?

There is a famous image of this story in the Vatican, painted by Raphael in 1511. We often imagine God speaking to Moses from out of the burning bush, and pass over the words of the text: "*the angel of the LORD appeared to him* in a flame of fire." In order to convey both the angel of the Lord in the flames and God himself calling out of the bush, Raphael paints two figures. Moses's face and body are bowed down before both. And the artist goes a step further. He turns the flying embers of the fiery bush into seraphim with blazing wings. An insightful artistic choice, because the name seraphim means "those who burn."

Raphael paints for us a theology in color. It is a theology of burning love, in which God seeks out his servant with patience and precision. Then, once he has our attention, he holds it long enough to draw us closer, long enough for the sparks of his glory to reach us and ignite a flame in our own souls. This is the work of the angels.

$\mathcal{B}$EFORE AND $\mathcal{B}$EHIND
Exodus 14:19–20; 23:20–22

The angel of God who was going before the Israelite army moved and went behind them; *and the pillar of cloud moved from in front of them and took its place behind them. It came between the army of Egypt and the army of Israel. And so the cloud was there with the darkness, and it lit up the night; one did not come near the other all night.*

I am going to send an angel in front of you, to guard you on the way and to bring you to the place that I have prepared. *Be attentive to him and listen to his voice; do not rebel against him, for he will not pardon your transgression; for my name is in him. But if you listen attentively to his voice and do all that I say, then I will be an enemy to your enemies and a foe to your foes.*

Marc Chagall (1887-1985) © ARS, NY
© RMN-Grand Palais / Art Resource, NY
The Crossing of the Red Sea. 1955. Oil on canvas, 216.5 x 146.0 cm.
AM 1988-80. Photo: Gérard Blot.

*I*F ASKED BY WHAT MIRACULOUS INSTRUMENTS the people of Israel were guided and protected in their exodus from Egypt, most of us would think of the "pillar of cloud by day and the pillar of fire by night" (Exod. 13:21–22). But there was another presence. According to Exodus 14, an angel scouted out the trail before the people, and when danger threatened them from behind (the chariots of Egypt), that same angel changed positions and became their rearguard. Some traditions have used these verses to identify the fiery and cloudy pillars as actual angels. If, as we have already found in earlier passages, angels must take a visible shape that is recognizable to the human eye in order to make their presence known, is it possible for them to take the form of nature's powers? Can they come in the breaking waves, in the moving clouds, in the rumbling thunder?

Marc Chagall painted a famous image of the passage through the Red Sea, depicting a giant angel leading the people through the parted waters, waving one arm and pointing the way with the other (*The Crossing of the Red Sea*, 1955). Did these same two colossal arms hold back the forces of Pharaoh and wrap themselves protectively around every man, woman, and child of Israel? The psalmist writes,

> For he will command his angels concerning you
> to guard you in all your ways. (Ps. 91:11)

This gives us the familiar understanding of the work of guardian angels. Like the pillars of cloud and fire, and like Chagall's gesticulating escort, such angels must be both sizable and powerful. These are not beings that we would gaze on eye to eye.

But their authority is founded on more than size and strength. In Exodus 23, we find another passage about an angel leading the people of Israel through the wilderness. We are told of the divine authority entrusted to this angel: "Hearken attentively to his voice and do all that *I* say." His voice is to be treated as the voice of God—"My name is in him," the Lord says. God's angel speaks and acts for God himself. In the fourth century, St. Hilary of Poitiers wrote that Israel was served by the angels during their entire forty-year sojourn—guided, protected, instructed, provided for. This is why Origen says to those who feel lost or confounded, "Do not waver at the solitude of the desert; it is during your sojourn in the tents that you will receive the manna from heaven and eat the bread of angels" (Origen, *Homilies on Numbers* 17.3). With nothing less than the strength and authority of God, the angels assist us through desert and flood alike. Behind the successful journey of each of God's children lie the unseen hands and sleepless labors of these heavenly ministers.

Balaam Stopped by the Angel. Early Christian fresco.
Credit: Scala / Art Resource, NY

A Man, a Donkey, and an Angel

Numbers 22:21–35

*So Balaam got up in the morning, saddled his donkey,
and went with the officials of Moab.*

*God's anger was kindled because he was going, and
the angel of the* Lord *took his stand in the road as his
adversary. Now he was riding on the donkey, and his
two servants were with him. The donkey saw the angel
of the* Lord *standing in the road, with a drawn sword
in his hand; so the donkey turned off the road, and
went into the field; and Balaam struck the donkey, to
turn it back onto the road. Then the angel of the* Lord
*stood in a narrow path between the vineyards, with a
wall on either side.*

When the donkey saw the angel of the Lord, *it
scraped against the wall, and scraped Balaam's foot
against the wall; so he struck it again. Then the angel
of the* Lord *went ahead, and stood in a narrow place,
where there was no way to turn either to the right
or to the left. When the donkey saw the angel of the*

LORD, *it lay down under Balaam; and Balaam's anger was kindled, and he struck the donkey with his staff. Then the* LORD *opened the mouth of the donkey, and it said to Balaam, "What have I done to you, that you have struck me these three times?" Balaam said to the donkey, "Because you have made a fool of me! I wish I had a sword in my hand! I would kill you right now!" But the donkey said to Balaam, "Am I not your donkey, which you have ridden all your life to this day? Have I been in the habit of treating you this way?" And he said, "No."*

Then the LORD **opened the eyes of Balaam, and he saw the angel of the** LORD **standing in the road, with his drawn sword in his hand;** *and he bowed down, falling on his face. The angel of the* LORD *said to him, "Why have you struck your donkey these three times? I have come out as an adversary, because your way is perverse before me. The donkey saw me, and turned away from me these three times. If it had not turned away from me, surely just now I would have killed you and let it live." Then Balaam said to the angel of the* LORD, *"I have sinned, for I did not know that you were standing in the road to oppose me. Now therefore, if it is displeasing to you, I will return*

home." The angel of the LORD *said to Balaam, "Go
with the men; but speak only what I tell you to speak."
So Balaam went on with the officials of Balak.*

THERE'S A BACKSTORY HERE. THE KING
of Moab is pressuring Balaam, a Mesopotamian
prophet of sorts, to go on a mission to curse the wandering
people of Israel before they have the chance to wage war
against the Moabites. God wants him to have no part in this
scheme, but when Balaam asks a second time, God seems
to relent and allow him to go with the king's henchmen.
As Balaam sets out, though, we have the strong impression
that God's first "you shall not go" should have been enough
for him. Even with God's apparent blessing, Balaam seems
to be overruling his own conscience. What happens next is
as fantastic as it is dramatic.

"The angel of the LORD took his stand in the road as
[Balaam's] *adversary.*" Here we are faced with a clear truth:
in order to guide us, angels must sometimes oppose us.
Balaam makes three attempts to lead his donkey around

the unseen obstacle, and each attempt leaves him more frustrated. God's angel counters every one of Balaam's moves, and the way gets nothing but tighter until it is impossible for Balaam to go any further. If the chief work of an angel is to bring God's message, then there is no mistaking this one: "Stop!"

But Balaam *does* miss the message, at least in part because he misses the messenger. Balaam sees only that the animal who has always done his bidding is now acting unruly and stubborn. Balaam does not see the upraised sword. Nor does he see the undoubtedly scowling face of the angel who holds it. How could he? A man whose focus on his own way has "blinded" him to God's ways isn't likely to perceive God's messenger either.

A simple animal, however, whose life is uncluttered by ambitions, ulterior motives, and guilt has no problem seeing the angel blocking the way. The Bible often presents God's creatures proclaiming his praise and glory (see the Psalms especially). Perhaps some have eyes as attuned to heaven as their voices. Doesn't it make you wonder what can be seen or at least perceived by the animal kingdom that we human beings miss, perhaps every day?

In his impatience, Balaam struck his donkey for its obstinate refusal to move forward. But who was the real stubborn one? Smart animal actually—choosing to face its master with a staff rather than an angel with a sword. Which one would you rather argue with?

Joking aside, this is a story of God opposing one man's misguided decisions, and using an angel to carry out his plan. We learn from it, too, that if God cannot get his servant to pay attention, he is not averse to using any means necessary to get the message across. Balaam's life was saved because an animal saw an angel and was afraid.

The Angel appearing to Araunah. Gerbrand van den Eeckhout
(1621-1674). Credit: Scala / Art Resource, NY

*A*N *A*NGEL *W*HO *S*EES *P*OSSIBILITY

Judges 6:11–14

*Now the angel of the L*ORD *came and sat under the oak at Ophrah,* which belonged to Joash the Abiezrite, as his son Gideon was beating out wheat in the wine press, to hide it from the Midianites. *The angel of the L*ORD *appeared to him and said to him,* "The LORD is with you, you mighty warrior." Gideon answered him, "But sir, if the LORD is with us, why then has all this happened to us? And where are all his wonderful deeds that our ancestors recounted to us, saying, 'Did not the LORD bring us up from Egypt?' But now the LORD has cast us off, and given us into the hand of Midian." Then the LORD turned to him and said, "Go in this might of yours and deliver Israel from the hand of Midian; I hereby commission you."

OLLOWING THE DAYS OF JOSHUA, AFTER the people of Israel entered the Promised Land and before the time of the Hebrew kings beginning with Saul—a period of about 350 years—Israel was ruled by a series of leaders known as "judges." These were divinely inspired heroes of the Jewish people, serving at one and the same time as prophetic voice, civilian magistrate, and military captain. The fledgling nation was only beginning to take shape, and these judges upheld the ancient covenant with God and defended the people against their enemies. Each in his or her own way (yes, there was a woman judge, the prophetess Deborah) was used by God to purge Israel of its idolatrous ways, deliver it from foreign oppression, and bring peace to the land. Gideon, a simple farmer from the smallest clan of the half-tribe of Manasseh, was one such judge. And we would know nothing of him were it not for the visitation of the angel of the Lord.

Are we beginning, in the call of Gideon, to see a familiar pattern? Once again, God's servant is going about his daily business when he is interrupted by a messenger from heaven, and does not know at first that the person standing before him is an angel. "Pray, sir," responds Gideon, to the angel's words. "*Sir*"? This is not the likely address for an angel of God. The angel could have overwhelmed Gideon by appearing in radiant splendor, looming over him with outstretched arms (wings?), wielding a flaming sword, and speaking with a voice of thunder. Sometimes this is just the sort of entrance that is called for. But as we read these stories, we find that each individual is treated in just that way—*individually*. Sometimes angels are immediately recognizable. Just as often, however, they are not. It seems an angel appearance relates directly to the particular person to whom they are appearing. There is no "one-size-fits-all" angelic annunciation . . . because people are not like that either.

While Gideon addressed the angel as "sir," the angel addressed Gideon as "you mighty man of valor." On that or any other day, certainly this would not have been Gideon's self-description. He was preparing his grain by hiding it in a winepress rather than risk being seen on an exposed hilltop. Against the marauding Midianites, he appears to assume he would stand helpless. The angel saw it differently, however. He saw something in Gideon that

Gideon did not yet see. He brought God's point of view to a meek farmer. Gideon was about to play a strategic role in answering the very question he'd asked the angel: "Where is the Lord?"

Burning Ones

Isaiah 6:1–7

In the year that King Uzziah died, I saw the Lord sitting on a throne, high and lofty; and the hem of his robe filled the temple. **Seraphs were in attendance above him; each had six wings: with two they covered their faces, and with two they covered their feet, and with two they flew.** *And one called to another and said:*

"Holy, holy, holy is the LORD *of hosts;*
the whole earth is full of his glory."

The pivots on the thresholds shook at the voices of those who called, and the house filled with smoke. And I said: "Woe is me! I am lost, for I am a man of unclean lips, and I live among a people of unclean lips; yet my eyes have seen the King, the LORD *of hosts!"* **Then one of the seraphs flew to me, holding a live coal that had been taken from the altar with a pair of tongs.** *The seraph touched my mouth with it and said: "Now that this has touched your lips, your guilt has departed and your sin is blotted out."*

*I*SAIAH'S EXPERIENCE IN THE TEMPLE ranks with the vision in Ezekiel 1 and the book of Revelation as one of the most dramatic, colorful, and sensational angelic encounters in all of Judeo-Christian history. No set of reflections on angels would be complete without it. All the more so because while most meetings involve an angel temporarily entering the world—bringing heaven to earth as it were—in this case, the prophet is temporarily entering heaven. Unsought, unforeseen, and certainly unnerving, Isaiah's meeting takes place at the throne of the One who sends all angels and to whom all angels return. There, Isaiah sees what the angels are really up to!

These verses contain the only use of the word "seraphim" in the Hebrew Bible—though these dazzling creatures appear a number of times in the book of Enoch, an ancient Hebrew text not included in the Bible. Among the angels, the seraphim stand with the cherubim nearest

Apse from the Church of Santa Maria d'Aneu (fresco), Master of Pedret,
(fl.1200) (attr. to) / Museu Nacional d'Art de Catalunya,
Barcelona, Spain / Photo © AISA / Bridgeman Images

to the throne of God and, like the "four living creatures" in Revelation 4, lead all of heaven in its unceasing song to God: "Holy, holy, holy."

The seraphim are the "burning ones," as we saw also in the story of Moses and the burning bush. As they purify Isaiah's mouth with fire in preparation for his prophetic ministry, they share their own passion for proclaiming the glory of God. In his study of the angelic order, *On the Celestial Hierarchy*, the sixth-century writer known as Pseudo-Dionysius cannot seem to find enough adjectives to describe the seraphim when he writes:

> The name *seraphim* clearly indicates their ceaseless and eternal revolution about Divine Principles, their heat and keenness, the exuberance of their intense, perpetual, tireless activity, and their elevative and energetic assimilation of those below, kindling them and firing them to their own heat, and wholly purifying them by a burning and all-consuming flame; and by the unhidden, unquenchable, changeless, radiant and enlightening power, dispelling and destroying the shadows of darkness.[2]

Thomas Aquinas identified their heat and energy as love. Their fire, he wrote, is due to an "excess of charity." They burn with ardor, and with that same burning zeal they worship God continually and purify the lives of God's people.

We are not angels and we never will be. Angels and human beings are entirely different creatures in the order of God's handiwork. But still, we can learn a great deal from them. We have already seen the example of their instant obedience to God's instructions, their resolute commitment to God's purposes, and their unwavering dedication to the good of human beings. In the seraphim of Isaiah's vision, we see another angelic attribute. Is it possible for our own lives to shine with charity? Can we too become burning lights?

Shadrach, Meshach and Abednego, the Three Youths in the Fiery Furnace of Nebuchadnezzur. 11th century CE. Byzantine Mosaic. Monastery Church, Hosios Loukas, Greece
Credit: Erich Lessing / Art Resource, NY

WHEN YOU WALK THROUGH FIRE

Daniel 3:24–28

*Then King Nebuchadnezzar was astonished and rose
up quickly. He said to his counselors, "Was it not
three men that we threw bound into the fire?" They
answered the king, "True, O king." He replied,* **"But I
see four men unbound, walking in the middle of the
fire, and they are not hurt; and the fourth has the
appearance of a god."**

*Nebuchadnezzar then approached the door of
the furnace of blazing fire and said, "Shadrach,
Meshach, and Abednego, servants of the Most High
God, come out! Come here!" So Shadrach, Meshach,
and Abednego came out from the fire. And the satraps,
the prefects, the governors, and the king's counselors
gathered together and saw that the fire had not had
any power over the bodies of those men; the hair of
their heads was not singed, their tunics were not
harmed, and not even the smell of fire came from
them. Nebuchadnezzar said,* **"Blessed be the God of**

Shadrach, Meshach, and Abednego, who has sent his angel and delivered his servants who trusted in him. They disobeyed the king's command and yielded up their bodies rather than serve and worship any god except their own God."

WHILE THE FIRE OF ISAIAH 6 IS HOLY and purifying, the fire of Nebuchadnezzar's furnace is purely unholy, set for a single evil purpose, to put to death three young men who refuse to break the first commandment: I am the Lord your God, you shall have no other gods before me. For their "crime" of faithfulness to God, they are condemned to be burned alive.

"Who is the god that will deliver you out of my hands?" asks the Babylonian king, convinced that nothing could resist his own power and that of the fiery furnace (Dan. 3:15). In the visible world, this may be true. There are any number of forces that can undo us. But if *what* we can see is as *far* as we can see, won't we miss seeing the hand of God? Under God's rule there is always more than meets the eye.

The faith of Shadrach, Meshach, and Abednego compels them to look beyond the king and beyond the furnace to another power, to an as-yet-unseen source of protection. "If it be so," they declare, "our God whom we serve is able to deliver us from the burning fiery furnace" (Dan. 3:17 RSV). They know God *can* save them; whether he *will* makes no difference in their decision to remain steadfast. The unseen God—the true and only irresistible power in the universe—will preserve them one way or another. Of this they are supremely confident.

Who, then, is this fourth "man" walking in the midst of the fire and having such power over the flames that not even the smell of smoke is left on the garments of his three young wards? Christian tradition has sometimes identified him with Christ—a hint at the incarnate presence of God, which would come generations later into a world smoldering in sin. Nebuchadnezzar identifies the man as God's angel—who "has the appearance of a god"—come to deliver his servants from death and to protect them from all harm. In order to do so, the angel descends directly into harm's way, appearing as just another victim offered to the flames. Such is the way of God's heavenly rescuers. They follow the example of their Master, who always says, "I will be *with* you."

The men were prepared to let flames consume their bodies rather than be unfaithful to God. He who has power over fire and heat, frost and cold, preserved their bodies by the hand of his angel. The Song of the Three Jews[3] includes further detail to the story, describing the young men walking around in the midst of the flames, praying, singing hymns, and blessing God for his goodness. From those writings the ancient church derived its practice of singing a canticle every morning that puts these lines into the voice of the divinely protected men.

> Bless the Lord, you angels of the Lord;
> > sing praise to him and highly exalt him forever. . . .
> Bless the Lord, fire and heat;
> > sing praise to him and highly exalt him forever.
> > (The Song of the Three Jews 37, 44
> > NEW OXFORD ANNOTATED BIBLE)

I Am Gabriel

Luke 1:8–19

*Once when [Zechariah] was serving as priest before God and his section was on duty, he was chosen by lot, according to the custom of the priesthood, to enter the sanctuary of the Lord and offer incense. Now at the time of the incense offering, the whole assembly of the people was praying outside. **Then there appeared to him an angel of the Lord, standing at the right side of the altar of incense.** When Zechariah saw him, he was terrified; and fear overwhelmed him. But the angel said to him, "Do not be afraid, Zechariah, for your prayer has been heard. Your wife Elizabeth will bear you a son, and you will name him John. You will have joy and gladness, and many will rejoice at his birth, for he will be great in the sight of the Lord. He must never drink wine or strong drink; even before his birth he will be filled with the Holy Spirit. He will turn many of the people of Israel to the Lord their God. With the spirit and power of Elijah he will go before him, to turn the hearts of parents to* *their children, and the disobedient to the wisdom of the righteous, to make ready a people prepared for the Lord." Zechariah said to the angel, "How will I know that this is so? For I am an old man, and my wife is getting on in years." The angel replied, **"I am Gabriel. I stand in the presence of God, and I have been sent to speak to you and to bring you this good news."***

$\mathcal{T}$HE DRAMATIC STORY OF GOD'S relationship with the world would not be possible without the presence and work of the angels. Throughout the Old Testament we have seen examples of the timely and pivotal role they play in bringing about God's purposes, protecting God's people, and announcing God's will. From the time of creation, angels have been both witnesses to and participants in God's plan for the redemption of the world. Moreover, their involvement is carried out in ways that are specifically designed to the needs and personalities of the individual men and women to whom they are sent. Because they are messengers *from* God, they direct the personal attention *of* God onto everyone they address

Alexander Ivanov (1806–1858). *Archangel Gabriel strikes Zacharias dumb*. End 1840s. Tretyakov Gallery, Moscow, Russia
Photo Credit: HIP / Art Resource, NY

and help. Angels are not heaven-bound strategists, making plans to help the human race while safely distant from its pain and trouble. Again and again the Bible records their presence among us, their presence *with* us. It is close, and it is personal. They even call us by name, as did Gabriel with the old priest Zechariah.

"Do not be afraid, Zechariah." With this personal address the events surrounding the coming of Christ commence—events that will include many, many angels. This angel knows Zechariah, his wife, Elizabeth, and their yet-to-be-conceived son, John. Despite the fact that Zechariah is in the temple to meet God, it is readily apparent that he is neither expecting nor ready to believe such a direct response to his prayers. Can we suppose that the angels *enjoy* surprising us with such news?

Zechariah's is not the only name we hear in this encounter. Scriptural accounts of angelic visitations do not usually include a personal introduction, but this one does: "I am Gabriel." The name comes from a Hebrew word meaning "man of God," sometimes translated "strength of God." We first encounter Gabriel by name when God addresses him by name and instructs him to reveal to the prophet Daniel the meaning of his visions (Dan. 8:15–17). From other writings, we have come to know Gabriel as one of the archangels, the chief messengers and warriors of the heavenly host.

Gabriel's message to Zechariah gives us one of the clearest of all explanations for the work of God's messengers: "I am Gabriel. I stand in the presence of God, and I have been sent to speak to you and to bring you this good news." The good news announced to Zechariah is only the introduction to the good news that is soon to be announced to the world. One of the mightiest of the angels comes to one of the weakest of men, and by this means God begins once again to accomplish his will. Origen said that the coming of Christ into the world was "a great joy for those to whom the care of men and nations had been entrusted." We cannot know when the angels first knew that joy, but we can dare to imagine that Gabriel's mission to Zechariah must have inspired some of it.

The Annunciation. Ca., Fra Angelico (1387-1455)
Copyright of the image Museo Nacional del Prado / Art Resource, NY

$\mathcal{H}$AIL, $\mathcal{O}$ $\mathcal{F}$AVORED $\mathcal{O}$NE
Luke 1:26–38

In the sixth month the angel Gabriel was sent by God to a town in Galilee called Nazareth, *to a virgin engaged to a man whose name was Joseph, of the house of David. The virgin's name was Mary. And he came to her and said, "Greetings, favored one! The Lord is with you." But she was much perplexed by his words and pondered what sort of greeting this might be. The angel said to her, "Do not be afraid, Mary, for you have found favor with God. And now, you will conceive in your womb and bear a son, and you will name him Jesus. He will be great, and will be called the Son of the Most High, and the Lord God will give to him the throne of his ancestor David. He will reign over the house of Jacob forever, and of his kingdom there will be no end." Mary said to the angel, "How can this be, since I am a virgin?" The angel said to her, "The Holy Spirit will come upon you, and the power of the Most High will overshadow you; therefore the child to be born will be holy; he will be called Son of*

God. And now, your relative Elizabeth in her old age
has also conceived a son; and this is the sixth month
for her who was said to be barren. For nothing will be
impossible with God." Then Mary said, "Here am I,
the servant of the Lord; let it be with me according to
your word." Then the angel departed from her.

*I*N ONE OF HIS SERMONS, A THIRD-CENTURY
bishop known as St. Gregory the Miracle-Worker
imagines the Annunciation from the angel Gabriel's point
of view. He imagines God directing Gabriel to approach
Mary gently: "Do not disturb or trouble the soul of the
Virgin. Greet her first with the voice of gladness and address
her, 'Hail, O favored one.'" The great archangel is filled
with awe and wonder at the news he is about to deliver.
Gregory says that Gabriel, on receiving God's instruction,
thinks to himself:

What has just been said is beyond comprehension.
He who is dreaded by the Cherubim, he who
cannot be looked on by the Seraphim, he who is

incomprehensible to all the heavenly powers—is
he saying that he will be connected in this way to a
virgin? Is he announcing that he will come in person?
Is he who condemned Eve eager to give Eve's daughter
such honor? This is certainly a fearful mystery.

Of all the angelic messages we encounter in the Bible,
the announcement to Mary that she will give birth to the
Son of God is certainly the most wonderful, and the most
mysterious. St. Gregory helps us to hear it in a fresh way,
news as startling to the hosts of heaven as to Mary. We can
picture Gabriel and Mary sharing a divine secret that gives
them both deep pause . . . and then deep joy.

In the famous fresco of the Annunciation painted by
fifteenth-century monk and master Fra Angelico, the scene
of Gabriel's visitation to Mary stands side by side with the
scene of Adam and Eve's banishment from the Garden.
The artist has taken his inspiration from the paradoxical
connection between the curse suffered by Adam and Eve
and the blessing brought by our Redeemer, a connection
so aptly expressed in the words of the *Exsultet*, an ancient
hymn for Easter.

> Father, how wonderful your care for us!
> How boundless your merciful love!
> To ransom a slave you gave away your Son.
> O happy fault, O necessary sin of Adam,
> which gained for us so great a Redeemer![4]

The artist pictures an angel presiding over the sorrowing Adam and Eve as they seem to limp out of Paradise. Their legs move as heavily as their hearts. At the center of the image the angel Gabriel makes a gentle bow to the Virgin Mary, who returns the humble gesture. They bend to one another, the maiden acknowledging the presence of God's messenger, the angel acknowledging the presence of God's Mother. A meeting of lowliness with lowliness, one servant speaking to another. This is the moment—and, once again, an angel stands in the center of it all—when Adam and Eve's expulsion begins to be reversed. Gabriel calls out, *Ave* (Hail), and Mary answers, *Fiat* (Let it be), and as their exchange echoes through heaven, the cherubim are motioned away from the gate, and the door to paradise begins to swing again upon its ancient hinges.

$\mathcal{I}$N THE $\mathcal{S}$TILLNESS OF THE $\mathcal{N}$IGHT

Matthew 1:18–21; 2:13–15, 19

*Now the birth of Jesus the Messiah took place in this way. When his mother Mary had been engaged to Joseph, but before they lived together, she was found to be with child from the Holy Spirit. Her husband Joseph, being a righteous man and unwilling to expose her to public disgrace, planned to dismiss her quietly. But just when he had resolved to do this, **an angel of the Lord appeared to him in a dream** and said, "Joseph, son of David, do not be afraid to take Mary as your wife, for the child conceived in her is from the Holy Spirit. She will bear a son, and you are to name him Jesus, for he will save his people from their sins."*

*   **Now after they had left, an angel of the Lord appeared to Joseph in a dream** and said, "Get up, take the child and his mother, and flee to Egypt, and remain there until I tell you; for Herod is about to search for the child, to destroy him." Then Joseph got up, took the child and his mother by night, and went*

Scene from the Life of Christ on the Ceiling: The Dream of St Joseph.
© Marie-Lan Nguyen / Wikimedia Commons / CC-BY 2.5

to Egypt, and remained there until the death of Herod. This was to fulfill what had been spoken by the Lord through the prophet, "Out of Egypt I have called my son."

When Herod died, an angel of the Lord suddenly appeared in a dream to Joseph in Egypt.

ERHAPS ONLY AS HE SLEPT WOULD JOSEPH be still enough to hear the angel's gentle whisper. Angels do not always come in the midst of a day's busy activity. Sometimes they must wait until we have shut down our racing thoughts and laid our stressed-out bodies to rest. Matthew tells us that Joseph was faced with a momentous decision: What was this man of honor and compassion to do with his betrothed now that she was bearing the child of another? He would have been justified in publicly renouncing her, canceling the marriage, and putting her to shame. And what of his own personal feelings of shame, of grief, and perhaps even of anger? He thinks he has come up with a solution—but it is not heaven's solution. So it is when Joseph is asleep and least able to resist the incredible that God's angel speaks to him an otherwise unthinkable thought.

He through whom the angels and all of creation came into being entrusts his own fragile birth in the flesh to these same angels. St. John Chrysostom said that in the period of the Old Covenant God set all things in motion through the angels, and that nothing was working out well. Nevertheless, God's work in the world was far from over. The angels now had their all-important role to play in the New Covenant, not the least of which was to recruit the support and obedience of some key players, like Mary and Zechariah . . . and Joseph. Was there a time when the angels were briefed on the incredible events to come but still, like the unknowing world, had to wait in expectation? Could this particular angel (some say it was Gabriel again) hardly wait until the night when he would visit Joseph and speak the name of Jesus into his ear?

Later, after the birth, another dream, another angel. Or perhaps it was the same angel as in Joseph's first dream. Then, "take Mary as your wife"—now, "flee to Egypt." Specific directions given for a specific purpose—to bring into this dark world the incarnate Light of heaven, and to keep that Light from being snuffed out at its most vulnerable beginnings. Joseph was to be the Father's chief ally in this effort, and the angel was to be his courier. The cupola of the Baptistery in Florence, Italy, from the thirteenth or fourteenth century, contains a mosaic detail representing this dream. Joseph is depicted asleep on a bare rock, his head propped up in one hand as if his slumber would be brief, breaking his watchfulness for only a few moments. His face is lifted toward heaven. The angel holding a scroll inscribed with the instruction to flee seems to be gliding down from the sky, his wings and robes virtually fluttering with excitement. Upon his own face appears the faintest of smiles as he lifts one hand and gestures to Joseph as if to say, "Pay attention, now, just as you did before. Here is the next step."

"The Seeing Shepherds", by Daniel Bonnell, www.BonnellArt.com

GLORY TO GOD

Luke 2:6–14

*While they were there, the time came for her to deliver
her child. And she gave birth to her firstborn son and
wrapped him in bands of cloth, and laid him in a
manger, because there was no place for them in the
inn.*

*In that region there were shepherds living in the
fields, keeping watch over their flock by night.* **Then
an angel of the Lord stood before them, and the
glory of the Lord shone around them,** *and they
were terrified. But the angel said to them, "Do not be
afraid; for see—I am bringing you good news of great
joy for all the people: to you is born this day in the city
of David a Savior, who is the Messiah, the Lord. This
will be a sign for you: you will find a child wrapped in
bands of cloth and lying in a manger."* **And suddenly
there was with the angel a multitude of the heavenly
host, praising God** *and saying, "Glory to God in the
highest heaven, and on earth peace among those whom
he favors!"*

*I*T SEEMS ALTOGETHER FITTING THAT THE birth of the Good Shepherd would be announced first to those who kept their flocks by night on the hills outside Bethlehem. Because we know none of them by name, these shepherds can represent us—simple, anonymous, unsuspecting, even unexpecting. They are greeted by a single angel whose sudden appearance— accompanied by the glorious light of heaven—is, in and of itself, too much for them to bear. This angelic encounter is quite unlike others where things seems quite ordinary and natural at first, like any other the conversation between two people (if there can be such a thing as an "ordinary" angelic visitation). As fearful as one angel had made the shepherds already, this was not sufficient for the announcement that night in Judea. The birth of the Son of God called for a multitude, a myriad, a countless throng of angels. Nor was it enough to hear words alone. This occasion called for music, and only the harmonies of heaven would suffice. Angels are messengers. They are also singers.

In a sermon on the prophet Ezekiel's vision of heaven, Origen depicts the angels waiting eagerly to descend to earth with the Son of God when the Word becomes flesh. He said:

> When the angels saw the Prince of the heavenly host descending among the places of earth, they entered by the way that he had opened, following their Lord and obeying the will of him who entrusted to their guardianship those who believe in him. The angels are in the service of your salvation. If he descended in a body, they have been granted to the Son of God to follow him. They say among themselves, "If he has put on mortal flesh, how can we remain doing nothing? Come, angels, let us all descend from heaven." That is why there was a multitude of the heavenly host praising and glorifying God when Christ was born. Everything is filled with angels.[5]

We usually think of this angelic choir as having been sent to announce the good news of Christ's birth to the shepherds. But what if that was only part of their purpose? What if they were there also to accompany their Lord as he made his way into this dark world, and to be present *for Jesus* when he was born in the flesh? What if they came, like so many heavenly midwives, to assist the Son of Man as he emerged from the womb of Mary into the hands of humanity? While some were singing, might others have been whispering something into the Savior's ear—something like, "Lord, we're here too. We all followed you down and, so long as you are here, we will be here too, whenever you need us"?

WATCHING . . .
WAITING . . . COMING

Matthew 4:1–11

Then Jesus was led up by the Spirit into the wilderness to be tempted by the devil. He fasted forty days and forty nights, and afterwards he was famished. The tempter came and said to him, "If you are the Son of God, command these stones to become loaves of bread." But he answered, "It is written,

> *'One does not live by bread alone, but by every word that comes from the mouth of God.'"*

Then the devil took him to the holy city and placed him on the pinnacle of the temple, saying to him, "If you are the Son of God, throw yourself down; for it is written,

> *'He will command his angels concerning you,'*
> *and 'On their hands they will bear you up,*
> *so that you will not dash your foot against a*
> *stone.'"*

Temptation on Mount, detail from Episodes from Christ's Passion and
Resurrection, reverse surface of Maestà of Duccio Altarpiece in Cathedral
of Siena, by Duccio di Buoninsegna (ca 1255–pre-1319), tempera on
wood, 1308-1311 / De Agostini Picture Library / Bridgeman Images

Jesus said to him, "Again it is written, 'Do not put the Lord your God to the test.'"

Again, the devil took him to a very high mountain and showed him all the kingdoms of the world and their splendor; and he said to him, "All these I will give you, if you will fall down and worship me." Jesus said to him, "Away with you, Satan! for it is written,

'Worship the Lord your God,
and serve only him.'"

Then the devil left him, and suddenly angels came and waited on him.

*T*HE WRITER TO THE HEBREWS SAYS THAT even as Jesus bears the full divinity of God, at the same time he takes on just as fully the limitations of human mortality. This, he says, makes Jesus the perfect source of help in our weakness: "We don't have a priest who is out of touch with our reality. He's been through weakness and testing, experienced it all—all but the sin" (Heb. 4:15 THE MESSAGE).

Jesus's handling of temptation in the wilderness is the model for our own spiritual conflicts with God's chief adversary—the antidote for the poisonous wound inflicted by the serpent in the Garden of Eden. A less familiar element of the story, mentioned in Matthew and in Mark (1:13), is the arrival of angels to care for Jesus at the end of this terrific fight. These heavenly beings would have known the Son of God in all his divine splendor. They would have known him as the *Logos*, the eternal Word of God, in whom and by whom and through whom all things have their being. From the beginning, their existence is entirely dependent on his. Yet here he is, self-confined by the limitations of human flesh, as hungry and thirsty as any man, weakened by his fasting, exhausted from his face-to-face encounter with the devil. Perhaps these angels are used to worshiping him in the glory of heaven; today, they are feeding him amid the dust of the earth . . . and he is depending on them.

One artistic image of this event presents Jesus at the center, standing on a mountain, at the moment he drives away the devil. Jesus is surrounded by the signs of his trial: the rocks, the towers, the earthly cities. After days of hunger and thirst in the wild, he has successfully fended off each of Satan's devious attacks. Unlike the tragic story of lost paradise where the devil took the form of a serpent, the Gospel writer does not tell us in what form the devil presented himself to Jesus. The artist directs our imagination by picturing Satan as a fallen angel complete with wings, now blackened and deformed. As he turns from Jesus, it is clear that he has been defeated, though not destroyed— Luke tells us he will wait for another opportunity to strike (4:13). That will be in another garden rather than the desert (see the following chapter in this book). Contrasted with the devil, two angels stand just behind Jesus, close by but not yet actively involved. The hand of one is raised in anticipation. They have been watching everything . . . and waiting.

If we have a Savior who is in touch with our reality, who has suffered the same weaknesses and tests, then surely we also share the same aid and comfort. Angels watch . . . and wait to come to our aid as well.

Blake, William (1757-1827). *The Agony in the Garden*, ca. 1799–1800.
Tempera on iron, 27.0 x 38.0 cm.
Photo Credit: Tate, London/ Art Resource, NY

At the Hour of Our Death

Luke 22:39–46

*He came out and went, as was his custom, to the
Mount of Olives; and the disciples followed him.
When he reached the place, he said to them, "Pray
that you may not come into the time of trial." Then
he withdrew from them about a stone's throw, knelt
down, and prayed, "Father, if you are willing, remove
this cup from me; yet, not my will but yours be done."*
**Then an angel from heaven appeared to him and
gave him strength.** *In his anguish he prayed more
earnestly, and his sweat became like great drops of
blood falling down on the ground. When he got up
from prayer, he came to the disciples and found them
sleeping because of grief, and he said to them, "Why
are you sleeping? Get up and pray that you may not
come into the time of trial."*

*T*HIS SCENE, FROM THE GOSPEL OF LUKE, begins the most remarkable days of the life of Jesus, including those most sacred three days (what the church calls the Paschal Triduum) of our Lord's passion, death, and resurrection—the accomplishment of Christ's redeeming sacrifice, the fulcrum of God's saving work in human history. From this point on, everything is changed.

It comes as no surprise that the angels should play an important role, assisting Jesus as he enters the path of his suffering, and later announcing his great victory when he defeats the "last enemy" (see 1 Cor. 15:26). Only a brief few years before at the inauguration of his public ministry, angels came to care for Jesus in the wilderness after he had battled with the temptations of the devil (as we read in the previous chapter). The angels helped ready Jesus for three years of unceasing sacrifice: teaching, healing, guiding, loving. As the Son of God lived among the human race, which would eventually betray and reject him, the race of angels was at his service. Now, as the Son of Man prepares for the brutal end of his life, he prays in the Garden of

Olives—an arboreal echo of the Garden of Eden—and once again receives heavenly help in his struggle.

In much of the artwork that depicts Jesus's agony at Gethsemane, an angel is shown as if descending from heaven and holding out a cup to Jesus. "Are you able to drink the cup that I am to drink?" Jesus once asked his ambitious followers, referring to the suffering he was destined to endure (Matt. 20:22). The angel who brings strength to Jesus also brings the bitter final draft of his sorrows. In some renditions, the cup of suffering is seen only in the anguished face of Jesus. The angel (sometimes it is more than one angel) is pictured *with* Jesus, embracing him, even enveloping him within the shadow of his wings. The angel is seen as the heaven-sent agent of God's love, the only way in which the Son can now know the presence of his Father.

In both interpretations of the event, the angel's support is not meant to *lighten* the burden Jesus is being asked to bear. Contained within the mystery of our Lord's passion is the profound truth that Jesus alone must bear the whole weight of human sin and its consequences. Not a grain of the burden can be shared with another. Not one single grain. What the angel can do is help Jesus *accept* his Father's will. The angel gives Jesus strength to take the cup and drink to the last drop. By Jesus's total self-giving for the purposes of grace, he wins us our salvation . . . and angels are there to help make it happen. What a debt we owe to these, our heavenly benefactors. Can we trust they will be there when our hour comes?

$\mathcal{A}$T THE $\mathcal{D}$AWN OF THE $\mathcal{D}$AY

Matthew 28:1–7; Mark 16:1–6

After the sabbath, as the first day of the week was dawning, Mary Magdalene and the other Mary went to see the tomb. And suddenly there was a great earthquake; **for an angel of the Lord, descending from heaven, came and rolled back the stone and sat on it.** *His appearance was like lightning, and his clothing white as snow. For fear of him the guards shook and became like dead men. But the angel said to the women, "Do not be afraid; I know that you are looking for Jesus who was crucified. He is not here; for he has been raised, as he said. Come, see the place where he lay. Then go quickly and tell his disciples, 'He has been raised from the dead, and indeed he is going ahead of you to Galilee; there you will see him.' This is my message for you."*

*T*HROUGH CENTURIES OF HUMAN HISTORY, angels had been dispatched by God to fulfill all kinds of duties and to deliver all kinds of messages. But from the time that death became the curse of our mortal condition ("You are dust, and to dust you shall return" [Gen. 3:19]), no duty or message had been more vital than the one carried out early that Sunday morning in a quiet garden just outside Jerusalem. In fact, every duty and every message of every angel had been one long preparation for the events of that day. Sitting atop the evidence of his handiwork—the rolled-back boulder door of a freshly opened tomb—an angel spoke the message above all messages: "He is not here; for he has been raised."

We are not told which angel received this ultimate assignment, which called for unimaginable solemnity and joy, as well as seismic strength. The first step of the job is to open the tomb, not because Jesus needs a way to get out but because a couple of women need a way to get in. They are to be the world's first witnesses to something heaven already knows. The last angel given gate duty was assigned

Giovanni Canavesio (15th century). *The Resurrection, scene from Christ's Passion*, fresco, 1492 / Chapelle Notre-Dame des Fontaines La Brigue
Photo Credit : Gianni Dagli Orti / The Art Archive at Art Resource, NY

to keep a way shut and sealed (remember Gen. 3:24). This angel (what if it is the same one?) is to remove the obstacle blocking our first new glimpse of paradise.

Matthew says that God's messenger is dressed for the occasion too, as bright as lightning and as white as snow. The sight is enough to paralyze the Roman guards charged with seeing that Jesus's body stays in the grave where it was put. They failed.

The resurrection of Jesus; the conquest of death; the defeat of the devil; the annulment of the curse; the redemption of all humanity: all of these are summed up in a single breath, with just a few words spoken by the mouth of an angel. We cannot fully equate human emotions with angelic feelings. Since they have no sin, the angels know nothing of fear and doubt, or the joy and lightheartedness of being forgiven. Nevertheless, Jesus spoke about the angels' great rejoicing over the repentance of a single sinner, so it is safe to say they know something of happiness and triumph (perhaps better than we do). Imagine for a moment, then, this angel's anticipation while awaiting the arrival of the women, and the sheer delight at seeing them as they first appeared on the pathway. Was there a thought like, "Wait till they see this—wait till they *hear* this!"? Even if only with our imaginations, it is helpful from time to time to look at these wondrous events through eyes different from our own. What does the angel see that morning? What is the view from atop that stone rolled away from the tomb?

Holy Women at the Tomb, 1894 (oil on canvas),
Maurice Denis (1870-1943) / Musee Maurice Denis,
St. Germain-en-Laye, France / Bridgeman Images

$\mathcal{H}$E $\mathcal{J}$S $\mathcal{R}$ISEN!
Luke 24:1–8; John 20:11–14

But on the first day of the week, at early dawn, they
came to the tomb, taking the spices that they had
prepared. They found the stone rolled away from the
tomb, but when they went in, they did not find the
body. While they were perplexed about this, **suddenly**
two men in dazzling clothes stood beside them. *The*
women were terrified and bowed their faces to the
ground, but the men said to them, "Why do you look
for the living among the dead? He is not here, but has
risen. Remember how he told you, while he was still
in Galilee, that the Son of Man must be handed over
to sinners, and be crucified, and on the third day rise
again."

But Mary stood weeping outside the tomb. As she
wept, she bent over to look into the tomb; **and she**
saw two angels in white, sitting where the body of
Jesus had been lying, one at the head and the other
at the feet. *They said to her, "Woman, why are you*

weeping?" She said to them, "They have taken away my Lord, and I do not know where they have laid him." When she had said this, she turned around and saw Jesus standing there, but she did not know that it was Jesus.

*T*HE APPEARANCE OF ANGELS AT THE Resurrection of Jesus is described differently in each of the four Gospels. In the previous chapter we considered the role of a single angel as recorded by Matthew and Mark (though with some differences between them). In this chapter we turn our attention to Luke and to John, each of whom writes of two angels; though again, each Gospel has its own particular emphasis.

Luke says that the angels appear as men, once again, apparently giving away their true identity only by the gleaming brightness of their garments—in the Greek, their apparel "shone like lightening." There's another interesting detail. In the other accounts, the angels stand at the entrance to the tomb and sit on the stone, or (in

John) wait where Jesus had lain. But in Luke's narrative, they appear to be identified more with the women than with the tomb—"two men *stood by them*." Their interest is in the welfare and encouragement of Jesus's mournful disciples. They who had "stood by" Jesus in the dark hours of his temptation and his agony now stand by his friends in their dark hours of grief and loss.

From the opening chapters, Luke gives significant attention to the role of the angels in the life of Christ. With Jesus "safely" risen from the dead, they now turn their attention to his followers. As in other accounts of angelic visitations, they must come close to us to bring the presence of God's love within human reach. On this morning, while consumed with fear after having lost their beloved Master, the women see the first sign of his presence on the faces of two angels. "Remember what he said to you," they say to their frightened listeners. This is a helpful way to think about the work of the angels on our behalf. In whatever way they can, by deed and by word, they *remind* us that Jesus is risen and alive—and that this is the final answer to everything.

John places the two angels in the empty tomb. They are not there to say to Mary, "Look what *we* have done." That is never an angel's message. Always the angels declare,

"Look what *God* has done." Pointing to their Lord is always their greatest joy. They wait for Jesus's friends, and when Mary appears at the door, they ask about the reason for her tears. They know that Jesus has risen and, in fact, they can see him standing right there behind Mary, even as she cries. Were there faint smiles on their faces, tingles of anticipation in their chests, as they waited for the precise moment, a moment they knew would come, when Mary would turn from them, and behold the One who stood behind her?

ℋ EAVEN'S 𝒲 ELCOME

Acts 1:3–5, 9–11

After his suffering he presented himself alive to [the apostles] by many convincing proofs, appearing to them during forty days and speaking about the kingdom of God. While staying with them, he ordered them not to leave Jerusalem, but to wait there for the promise of the Father. "This," he said, "is what you have heard from me; for John baptized with water, but you will be baptized with the Holy Spirit not many days from now."

*When he had said this, as they were watching, he was lifted up, and a cloud took him out of their sight. While he was going and they were gazing up toward heaven, **suddenly two men in white robes stood by them.** They said, "Men of Galilee, why do you stand looking up toward heaven? This Jesus, who has been taken up from you into heaven, will come in the same way as you saw him go into heaven."*

*J*N OUR OPENING CHAPTER, WE EXPLORED the first appearance in the Bible of an angel. The cherubim served God by barring the way to the Garden of Eden, preventing Adam and Eve from returning to Paradise. There we noted that by acting as God's own hand blocking humanity's way, they point us toward our only hope of return: "the mercy of God who will make the way himself."

Gregory of Nyssa, a fourth-century bishop and theologian who is honored by both the East and the West, said that the fall of Adam and Eve broke God's intended communion between heaven and earth by snatching men and women away from the company of the angels. Since then, the angels have watched and waited, longing for humanity's restoration. With the ascension of Christ comes the accomplishment of all that the Gospel promises and thereby the fulfillment of all their hopes. "When grace has reunited men and angels," wrote Gregory, "[the angels] will break forth into a great hymn of praise."[6] With Gregory we can wonder: if a countless host of angels sang at the quiet birth of the Savior, what must have been the sound in heaven at his glorious return?

Ascension of Christ, Giotto di Bondone (1266-1336)
Credit: Alfredo Dagli Orti / The Art Archive at Art Resource, NY

The great fourteenth-century Florentine master Giotto di Bondone made a series of twenty-four fresco panels for the now-famous Scrovegni Chapel in Padua. They portray the life of Christ, and the second to last panel, just before the image of Pentecost, depicts the Ascension. Faithful to the biblical account, the artist depicts the apostles and Mary (see Acts 1:14) gathered on the hilltop from which Jesus has just ascended. While two angels instruct them to stop gazing into the sky and instead to go about their God-given duties, Giotto imagines more angels welcoming Jesus back from his earthly sojourn. The angels and archangels and all the host of heaven have obtained what they were always waiting for: the reunion of heaven and earth, the return of man and woman to the dignified condition in which and for which they were created.

The angels, who once blocked our way from the presence of God, now do everything in their power to help us ascend to paradise. In Jesus's ascension to the Father is our ascension, just as in his crucifixion we also were crucified, dead, buried, and raised again. The curse of exile is reversed. God's promise is kept. The gate is reopened, and Jesus is the first to enter. But he is not the last. The angels stand ready to usher *us* in too, when our time comes.

$\mathcal{A}$ $\mathcal{G}$UARDIAN $\mathcal{A}$NGEL
AT $\mathcal{W}$ORK

Acts 12:1–11

It was about this time that King Herod arrested some who belonged to the church, intending to persecute them. He had James, the brother of John, put to death with the sword. When he saw that this met with approval among the Jews, he proceeded to seize Peter also. This happened during the Festival of Unleavened Bread. After arresting him, he put him in prison, handing him over to be guarded by four squads of four soldiers each. Herod intended to bring him out for public trial after the Passover.

So Peter was kept in prison, but the church was earnestly praying to God for him.

The night before Herod was to bring him to trial, Peter was sleeping between two soldiers, bound with two chains, and sentries stood guard at the entrance. **Suddenly an angel of the Lord appeared and a light shone in the cell.** *He struck Peter on the side and woke him up. "Quick, get up!" he said, and the chains* *fell off Peter's wrists. Then the angel said to him, "Put on your clothes and sandals." And Peter did so. "Wrap your cloak around you and follow me," the angel told him. Peter followed him out of the prison, but he had no idea that what the angel was doing was really happening; he thought he was seeing a vision. They passed the first and second guards and came to the iron gate leading to the city. It opened for them by itself, and they went through it. When they had walked the length of one street, suddenly the angel left him.*

Then Peter came to himself and said, "Now I know without a doubt that the Lord has sent his angel and rescued me from Herod's clutches and from everything the Jewish people were hoping would happen." (NIV)

*L*UKE'S RECORD OF THE DELIVERANCE of Peter from prison is a fascinating story in its own right, and it also introduces an idea that has been treasured and handed down through centuries of Judeo-Christian tradition: guardian angels. In this chapter of the

The Liberation of St. Peter from Prison, detail. Fresco.
Raphael (Raffaello Sanzio) (1483-1520).
Credit: Scala / Art Resource, NY

Acts of the Apostles, tragic circumstances are mixed with an almost humorous account of Peter's experience with one of these divinely appointed protectors.

The persecution of the early church had begun in earnest and, after Stephen (Acts 7), one of the first to fall victim to its cruelty, was James the brother of John. At the hands of Herod Agrippa (grandson of Herod the Great), it looked as if Peter would be next. All that the church could do was to pray . . . which was apparently enough. In his description of what comes next, Luke is very particular about the details, which serve to emphasize the impossibility of Peter's situation as well as the miraculous method of his deliverance. And it does not escape Luke that Peter will languish in prison on the Passover, the very day that the Jewish people are celebrating their liberation from slavery in Egypt.

Herod has taken every precaution to prevent Peter's rescue or escape—clearly never considering that, like the fiery furnace of the three men in the book of Daniel (see chapter on Dan. 3), Peter's chamber might have room for a visitor. Step by step, Luke leads us through the angel's method: illuminating the room; rousing Peter with a smack to his side; releasing the chains; instructing Peter on how to get dressed (can you see the apostle fumbling for his sandals in a barely woken daze?); leading him past the guards; remotely opening the gate; and, finally, delivering Peter safely to the nighttime street, where the angel (as usual, dare we say?) promptly disappears.

Clearly, Luke wants us to see both the hand of the church at work through its prayers and intercessions, and the hand of God at work through the angel's oversight. It is the tender condescension, the careful and personal nature, of this oversight that leads many to say this is Peter's guardian angel. (For other examples of guardian angels, see Matt. 18:10; Gen. 48:16; and the wonderful story of Tobias and the archangel Raphael in Tobit 5.) Apparently, by the apostles' time, it was thought that a guardian angel took on the characteristics of his charge, for Peter's indignant friends conclude that it cannot be Peter standing outside their door but rather "his angel" (Acts 12:15).

Like many other early church teachers, St. Basil said that some angels are responsible for the welfare of individual men and women. An angel guards each believer's soul, he says, acting as teacher and shepherd. The apostle Peter's guardian angel certainly fulfills such a duty on that Passover night in Jerusalem.

$\mathcal{D}$IVINE $\mathcal{R}$EMINDERS

Acts 27:18–25

*We were being pounded by the storm so violently
that on the next day they began to throw the cargo
overboard, and on the third day with their own hands
they threw the ship's tackle overboard. When neither
sun nor stars appeared for many days, and no small
tempest raged, all hope of our being saved was at last
abandoned.*

*Since they had been without food for a long time,
Paul then stood up among them and said, "Men, you
should have listened to me and not have set sail from
Crete and thereby avoided this damage and loss. I
urge you now to keep up your courage, for there will
be no loss of life among you, but only of the ship. **For
last night there stood by me an angel of the God
to whom I belong and whom I worship,** and he
said, 'Do not be afraid, Paul; you must stand before
the emperor; and indeed, God has granted safety to
all those who are sailing with you.' So keep up your*

An Angel Appears to Paul at Sea,
Image copyright www.StainedGlassInc.com

courage, men, for I have faith in God that it will be exactly as I have been told."

JUST AS SOME ANGELS ARE ENTRUSTED with the care of individual souls, some are charged with the protection of the church—God's chief messenger of the Gospel. One third-century pastor and theologian, Hippolytus of Rome, likened these angels to sailors who stand on both sides of a sailing ship, watching for and defending against all harm. Perhaps at no time was this aid needed more than when, in her infancy, the church was first beginning to speak to the world.

The Bible's record of the church's fledgling growth, the Acts of the Apostles, recounts numerous occasions when angels are sent to assist and to direct the first Christians. From time to time, these heavenly warriors dispatched enemies of the church, as with Herod in Luke 12:21–24, thereby allowing the Word of God to, as Luke puts it, grow and multiply. More often, their assignment is far less violent, though no less vital: opening prison doors so the apostles can preach (Acts 5:17–25); giving Philip his next assignment (8:26); telling Cornelius the centurion to send for Simon Peter (10:1–8); releasing Peter from prison (12:6–11); calling Paul to preach in Macedonia (16:9); and finally here, near the end of the record, encouraging Paul in the face of danger.

Though under arrest, Paul knows God's purpose is being fulfilled through his difficult circumstances. By *not* being miraculously freed, Paul will be taken to Rome as a prisoner. There he will be allowed to preach and teach, "with all boldness and without hindrance," as the final verse of Acts tells us (28:31). With the angels as our protectors, we must not think mistakenly that harm should never come to us. God's purposes, which are always motivated by love, will sometimes include suffering. Then the angels will come not to save but to support—as they did Jesus in the Garden of Gethsemane—and to encourage us in the midst of our pain.

Shortly after his arrest, Paul heard the Lord say that, eventually and inevitably, he would bear witness to Christ in the city of Rome, just as he had been doing in Jerusalem (Acts 23:11). Two years later, lost at sea in the middle of the night, an angel came to Paul, reminding him that God's plan had not changed. Neither the foolishness of the crew nor the power of the storm would drive God's intention for Paul off course. With that reminder came the assurance that, though the ship and all the cargo would be lost, every soul on board would be saved—souls for whom the apostle had been praying. In the darkness of that stormy night—or any other kind of night for that matter—it is the angel's job to shed fresh light on promises that might otherwise be lost in life's turbulent seas.

WORSHIP GOD

Revelation 1:1–3

*The revelation of Jesus Christ, which God gave him to show his servants what must soon take place; **he made it known by sending his angel to his servant John,** who testified to the word of God and to the testimony of Jesus Christ, even to all that he saw. Blessed is the one who reads aloud the words of the prophecy, and blessed are those who hear and who keep what is written in it; for the time is near.*

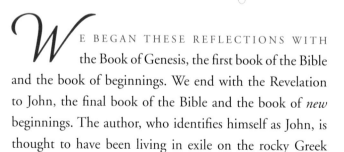

W E BEGAN THESE REFLECTIONS WITH the Book of Genesis, the first book of the Bible and the book of beginnings. We end with the Revelation to John, the final book of the Bible and the book of *new* beginnings. The author, who identifies himself as John, is thought to have been living in exile on the rocky Greek island of Patmos, during a period of persecution in the

Commentary on the Apocalypse. Spain, 10th CE. Author: Beato de Liebana. Location: Monasterio-Biblioteca-Coleccion, San Lorenzo Del Escorial, Madrid, Spain. Photo Credit : Album / Art Resource, NY

early church (1:9–10). The opening word of the Greek text, *apokalypsis*, means to uncover or disclose, suggesting a veil being lifted to reveal something that would otherwise remain hidden from view. From the very start of his report, the writer considers himself to be only a witness to, rather than a participant in, the things he is being shown. He knows that whatever understanding he can convey is made known to him by someone else. And it all starts with the sending of an angel.

The book of Revelation accounts for more than one-quarter of the references to angels in the entire Bible. They instruct John and they lead him; they tell him and they show him. John sees and hears angels in all aspects of their duties: they deliver God's acts and words of both judgment and mercy to the earth; they worship and praise in the courts of heaven; they welcome the redeemed and abandon the reprobate; they proclaim God's reign and defeat God's enemy; they shed light on the earth and bring the plagues of wrath; they protect, they fight, and they sing. They emerge always at the ready, unwaveringly dedicated to executing whatever tasks they are assigned. From fantastic scene to even more fantastic scene, the angels in the book of Revelation appear focused on a singular purpose: to serve Almighty God.

Thus we end where we began. The first priority of the heavenly host is to serve at the pleasure of their Creator and Lord—angels do God's bidding, not ours. This should give us pause as well as great hope: pause as we confront our all-too-human penchant for thinking everything is about us; and great hope because, by their dedication to God's will, the angels are forever dedicated to God's will *for us*. If we dare take John as our example, then ultimately what the angels do for us is reveal God. For it is never the intention of the angels that our attention should rest on them. They are always intermediaries pointing us beyond themselves, pointing us to Jesus. Toward the conclusion of his vision on the island of Patmos, just before he is overwhelmed with the consuming splendor of heaven's glory, John falls down at the feet of the angel who has been showing him the revelation from the beginning (Rev. 22:8–9). But his heavenly guide will have none of it. "You must not do that!" exclaims the angel. "I am a fellow servant with you and your comrades. . . . Worship God."

NOTES

1 Pseudo-Dionysius the Areopagite, *On the Celestial Hierarchy* 6 (in *Orthodox Life* 27, no. 6 [1977]).

2 Pseudo-Dionysius the Areopagite, *On the Celestial Hierarchy* 7.1 (in *Esotericism, Religion, and Nature*, ed. Arthur Versluis et al. [Minneapolis: North American Academic Press, 2010], 165–66).

3 The Prayer of Azariah and the Song of the Three Jews 28–68 (in *New Oxford Annotated Bible*, ed. Michael Coogan et al., 4th ed. [Oxford: Oxford University Press, 2010]).

4 Excerpt from the English translation of *The Roman Missal* (International Commission on English in the Liturgy Corporation, 2010).

5 Origen, quoted in Jean Daniélou, *The Angels and Their Mission; According to the Fathers of the Church* (Westminster, MD: Newman Press, 1957), 31.

6   Gregory of Nyssa, *Homily on Psalm 9*, quoted in Jean
     Daniélou, *The Angels and Their Mission* (Westminster,
     MD: Newman Press, 1957), 127.

ABOUT PARACLETE PRESS

Who We Are

Paraclete Press is a publisher of books, recordings, and DVDs on Christian spirituality. Our publishing represents a full expression of Christian belief and practice—from Catholic to Evangelical, from Protestant to Orthodox.

We are the publishing arm of the Community of Jesus, an ecumenical monastic community in the Benedictine tradition. As such, we are uniquely positioned in the marketplace without connection to a large corporation and with informal relationships to many branches and denominations of faith.

What We Are Doing

PARACLETE PRESS BOOKS | Paraclete publishes books that show the richness and depth of what it means to be Christian. Although Benedictine spirituality is at the heart of who we are and all that we do, we publish books that reflect the Christian experience across many cultures, time periods, and houses of worship. We publish books that nourish the vibrant life of the church and its people.

We have several different series, including theww best-selling Paraclete Essentials and Paraclete Giants series of classic texts in contemporary English; Voices from the Monastery—men and women monastics writing about living a spiritual life today; our award-winning Paraclete Poetry series as well as the Mount Tabor Books on the arts; best-selling gift books for children on the occasions of baptism and first communion; and the Active Prayer Series that brings creativity and liveliness to any life of prayer.

MOUNT TABOR BOOKS | Paraclete's newest series, Mount Tabor Books, focuses on the arts and literature as well as liturgical worship and spirituality, and was created in conjunction with the Mount Tabor Ecumenical Centre for Art and Spirituality in Barga, Italy.

PARACLETE RECORDINGS | From Gregorian chant to contemporary American choral works, our recordings celebrate the best of sacred choral music composed through the centuries that create a space for heaven and earth to intersect. Paraclete Recordings is the record label representing the internationally acclaimed choir Gloriæ Dei Cantores, praised for their "rapt and fathomless spiritual intensity" by *American Record Guide*; the Gloriæ Dei Cantores Schola, specializing in the study and performance of Gregorian chant; and the other instrumental artists of the Gloriæ Dei Artes Foundation.

Paraclete Press is also privileged to be the exclusive North American distributor of the recordings of the Monastic Choir of St. Peter's Abbey in Solesmes, France, long considered to be a leading authority on Gregorian chant.

PARACLETE VIDEO | Our DVDs offer spiritual help, healing, and biblical guidance for a broad range of life issues including grief and loss, marriage, forgiveness, facing death, bullying, addictions, Alzheimer's, and spiritual formation.

Learn more about us at our website:
www.paracletepress.com or phone us
toll-free at 1.800.451.5006

SCAN
TO
READ
MORE

Also Available from Paraclete Press. . .

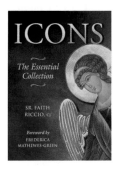

ICONS:
The Essential Collection
by Sr. Faith Riccio

ISBN 978-1-61261-831-9, $16.99, Hardcover

Icons are an invitation to go beyond our world; to take a moment to look as through a window into heaven. This gift book has over sixty full color icon images, each paired with a Scripture and an inspirational word. "The images in this book will present to us, over and over, that mystery of personhood, as we encounter the face of Christ and of those who loved him" —From the foreword by Frederica Mathewes-Green

CHANTS OF ANGELS
Gloriæ Dei Cantores

ISBN 978-1-55725-925- 7, $18.95, CD
Running time 55 minutes

"Be transported to a place of timeless eternal beauty" —Kansas City Star

These ancient melodies of the church tell the stories of heavenly guardians, guides and friends. The Chants of Angels allows listeners to simply close their eyes, and be surrounded by these songs of prayer comfort.

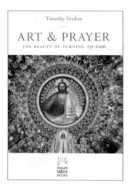

ART AND PRAYER:
The Beauty of Turning to God
Timothy Verdon

ISBN 978-1-61261-572-1, Hardcover, $34.99

Renowned art historian Timothy Verdon
explores how sacred art can teach us to pray
in this stunningly beautiful, richly illustrated
book. "Images put before believers can in fact
teach them how to turn to God in prayer . . ."
This is the "art of prayer," when faith and prayer
become creative responses by which the creatures learn to relate to the Creator.
Read this book slowly and let the words and the art inform your meditations. A
perfect gift for anyone who loves sacred art.

> "A visual and verbal feast for contemplation and study."
> *Publishers Weekly*
> December 2014

Available through your local bookseller
or through Paraclete Press:
www.paracletepress.com; 1-800-451-5006